The Nile River

By Allan Fowler

Consultant
Linda Cornwell, Learning Resource Consultant,
Indiana Department of Education

Children's Press®
A Division of Grolier Publishing
New York   London   Hong Kong   Sydney
Danbury, Connecticut

Visit Children's Press® on the Internet at:
http://publishing.grolier.com

Designer: Herman Adler Design Group

Library of Congress Cataloging-in-Publication Data

Fowler, Allan.
    The Nile River / by Allan Fowler.
      p. cm. — (Rookie read-about geography)
    Includes index.
    Summary: Introduces the world's longest river, describing its origin, tributaries,
animal life, and the different countries through which it flows.
    ISBN 0-516-21559-0 (lib. bdg.) 0-516-26559-8 (pbk.)
    1. Nile River—Juvenile literature. [1. Nile River.] I. Title. II. Series.
DT115.F685   1999   98-43962
  916.2—dc21   CIP
                                                 AC

GROLIER
PUBLISHING

The Nile is the longest river in the world.

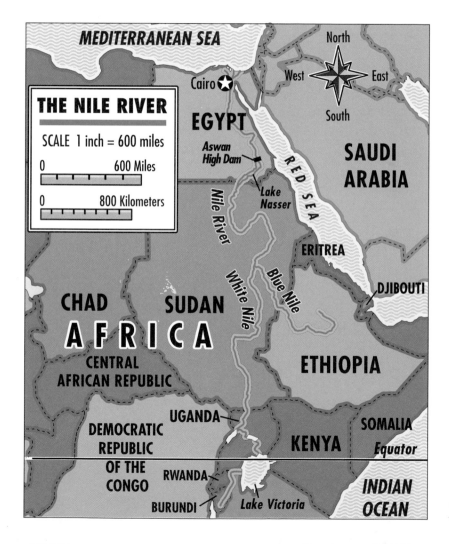

THE NILE RIVER

SCALE 1 inch = 600 miles

0   600 Miles

0   800 Kilometers

MEDITERRANEAN SEA

North
West   East
South

Cairo ★

EGYPT

Aswan High Dam

Lake Nasser

Nile River

RED SEA

SAUDI ARABIA

ERITREA

White Nile

Blue Nile

DJIBOUTI

CHAD

SUDAN

AFRICA

CENTRAL AFRICAN REPUBLIC

ETHIOPIA

UGANDA

DEMOCRATIC REPUBLIC OF THE CONGO

KENYA

SOMALIA

Equator

RWANDA

BURUNDI

Lake Victoria

INDIAN OCEAN

The Nile River is more than 4,000 miles long. It flows through Africa, from south to north.

The Nile begins in the country of Burundi. It enters and leaves big Lake Victoria.

Lake Victoria

Fishermen's huts in a swamp in Sudan

Then the Nile crosses
another country called
Sudan. There it flows
through swamps.

Plants called papyrus
(puh-PYE-ruhss) grow
in the swamps.

Long ago, people made
paper for writing from
papyrus.

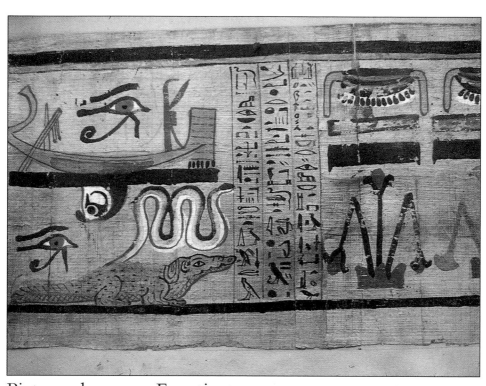

Pictures drawn on Egyptian papyrus

The next part of the river is called the White Nile. Another part of the river, the Blue Nile, begins in the country of Ethiopia.

Falls on the Blue Nile

Blue Nile   White Nile

The Blue Nile flows through grasslands. The White and Blue Nile meet in Sudan. They become one river.

12

From there, the river is called the Nile. It passes through desert.

Boats cannot sail on this part of the river.

There are many rocks and the water is rough.

At Aswan, in Egypt, the Aswan High Dam was built across the Nile.

The water behind the dam formed Lake Nasser.

It is one of the largest man-made lakes in the world.

Aswan High Dam

Taking apart one of the temples

Lake Nasser would
have covered two
ancient temples.

So the temples were
taken apart and put
back together on
higher ground.

There are many farms along the Nile between Aswan and the sea.

The Nile used to flow over its banks every year.

The waters often covered homes and farms.

Farmers in a wheat field

Now the dam stops the
river from overflowing.

It provides water to keep
the soil moist all year long.

Farmers grow cotton,
corn, rice, wheat, beans,
fruits, and vegetables.

Crocodiles live in the Nile.

A Nile crocodile

Nile perch

So do turtles, snakes,
Nile perch, catfish,
and eels.

The Nile passes the great city of Cairo, in Egypt.

Then the river splits into two branches.

Cairo, Egypt

Mediterranean Sea

Nile River Delta

Branch of Nile

Branch of Nile

Nile River

Space Shuttle

A view of the Nile River Delta from a space shuttle

Bits of rock and soil are carried by the river.

They pile up near its mouth to form new land called a delta.

Both of the Nile branches flow through the delta.

At last the Nile flows into the Mediterranean Sea.

Mediterranean Sea

Words You Know

Cairo

crocodile

dam

delta

30